Jacques Cartier

and the Exploration of Canada

Explorers of New Worlds

Explorers of New Worlds

EAST WINDSOR INTERMEDIATE SCHOOL

Jacques Cartier

and the Exploration of Canada

B
CAR

Daniel E. Harmon

Chelsea House Publishers
Philadelphia

Prepared for Chelsea House Publishers by:
OTTN Publishing, Stockton, N.J.

CHELSEA HOUSE PUBLISHERS
Production Manager: Pamela Loos
Art Director: Sara Davis
Director of Photography: Judy L. Hasday
Managing Editor: James D. Gallagher
Senior Production Editor: J. Christopher Higgins
Series Designer: Keith Trego
Cover Design: Forman Group

3 5 7 9 8 6 4 2

Library of Congress Cataloging-in-Publication Data

Harmon, Daniel E.
    Jacques Cartier and the exploration of
        Canada / Daniel E. Harmon.
        p.   cm. – (Explorers of new worlds)
Includes bibliographical references and index.
Summary: Describes the life and travels of Jacques
Cartier, the sixteenth century French navigator who
made three voyages to what is today known as Canada,
in search of a northwest passage to China.
ISBN 0-7910-5958-8 (hc) – ISBN 0-7910-6168-X (pbk.)
1. Cartier, Jacques, 1491-1557–Juvenile literature.
2. Explorers–America–Biography–Juvenile literature.
3. Explorers–France–Biography–Juvenile literature.
4. Canada–Discovery and exploration–Juvenile literature. 5. Canada–History to 1763 (New France)–Juvenile
literature. [1. Cartier, Jacques, 1491-1557. 2. Explorers.
3. Canada–Discovery and exploration. 4. Canada–History to 1763 (New France).] I. Title. II. Series.

E133.C3.H27 2000
971.4'012–dc21   00-043075

Contents

Sauvage Iroquois

This colorful drawing of an Iroquois is from a 16th-century French book on Canada. Jacques Cartier and his men encountered the Iroquois when they sailed up the St. Lawrence River.

A Boy Looks Seaward

I

To the French explorers under the command of Jacques Cartier, the strange people of the New World seemed wild, primitive, and utterly poor. These Native Americans looked like characters in a dream . . . or creatures from the incredible tales deep-sea fishermen told in dockside taverns.

Actually, they were members of the *Iroquois confederacy*, a collection of tribes living along the St. Lawrence River in what is today the Canadian *province* of Quebec. By 1535, several French expeditions and countless fishing fleets had crossed the Atlantic and encountered Native

Americans, but the sight of these so-called savages captivated the men on this, Cartier's second mission to the New World. One of them wrote:

> The inhabitants of the country clothe themselves with the skins of certain wild beasts, but very miserably. In winter they wear hose and shoes made of wild beasts' skins, and in summer they go barefooted. . . .
>
> They dig their grounds with certain pieces of wood as big as half a sword, on which ground groweth their corn. . . .
>
> The women of that country do labor much more than the men, as well in fishing . . . as in tilling and husbanding their grounds. . . . When as the snow and ice lyeth on the ground, they take great store of wild beasts, as fawns, stags, bears, martens, hares, and foxes . . . whose flesh they eat raw.

Cartier and his followers were the first Europeans to encounter the Iroquois along the St. Lawrence, and such reports of wearing animal skins for clothes and eating raw meat and fish must have turned delicate stomachs in the king's court back home. In the coming centuries, however, the French and Indians would learn each other's ways. They would fight–both as friends and foes. And in time, the French would replace the Native Americans as inhabitants of the fertile St. Lawrence Valley. Soon, the French adventurers in the new land would adopt many of the peculiar Native American ways as their own. They would have to if they wanted to survive the hardships of the wilderness.

Jacques Cartier was born in 1491, historians believe, in St. Malo. This is an island seaport on the coast of Brittany, a province in northwestern France. If you look at a map of France, you will find the Gulfe de St. Malo (Gulf of St. Malo) below the Channel Islands at the lower end of the English Channel.

For many years St. Malo had been respected for its skilled fishers and sailors. Some of these hardy seafarers constantly looked for new waters to fish and for new lands and riches as well.

Jacques grew up with the smell of salt air in his nostrils and tales of adventure in his head. As a boy, he must have been curious about what lay beyond the gulf's gray horizon to the north-northwest. As a young man he traveled to Dieppe, another French seaport about 150 miles up the English Channel, and there he learned the art of navigation.

In 1492, the year after Cartier was born, Christopher Columbus sailed west from Spain across the

Atlantic Ocean and discovered a strange land. Later explorers determined that this was a great landmass. We know today that this great mass of land was the twin continents of North and South America. But in the early 1500s, European explorers were trying to find a route to sail from Europe around the world to the Orient, where they could trade for valuable *spices*. They knew only that this New World was in their way.

French sea captains soon became interested in the New World. Soon after Columbus's voyages, French fishermen began braving the Atlantic to peer along the upper coast of North America at what is today the Maritime Provinces of eastern Canada. The fishermen's voyages across the Atlantic were bold adventures, for many Europeans were superstitious, and seamen told strange tales of ferocious monsters that lived in the North Atlantic. In fact, some seafarers were convinced Satan himself lived in the mysterious New World.

However, the fishermen couldn't resist the lure of the exciting fishing waters known as the Grand Banks. Here, sailors of the day claimed, the schools of fish—especially cod—were so thick they slowed the progress of sailing ships!

The year after Jacques Cartier was born, Christopher Columbus made his first voyage across the Atlantic. Columbus had been searching for a route to the Indies. Instead, he found a "New World"—the Americas.

Some of their countrymen, however, journeyed to this area with other purposes in mind. French **corsairs** had begun attacking Spanish towns in the New World. They captured Spanish cargo ships, known as **galleons**, that were bringing gold and other treasures back to Europe.

Meanwhile, a new breed of French sea commander was eyeing the waters to the north. These men wanted to find the **Northwest Passage**, a water route that ships could follow through the New World and on to China.

In 1497 John Cabot, an Italian sailing for England, reached Newfoundland, a large island that is

The Newfoundland coast was discovered in 1497 by an Italian sailor named John Cabot. In 1498 Cabot sailed from Europe intending to return to Newfoundland, but he was never heard from again.

the cold eastern end of today's nation of Canada. Cabot was one of the first to report the great schools of codfish in the **Grand Banks** off the Newfoundland coast. These stories impelled the fishers of St. Malo and other French ports to weather the chilly, stormy North Atlantic to find better fishing.

We don't know for certain, but Jacques Cartier

probably sailed aboard vessels in the St. Malo fishing fleet when he was a young man. He may have made the long, dangerous trip to the Grand Banks. We know Cartier spoke Portuguese, so he may also have been aboard one of the Portuguese ships that explored the coast of South America during this period. Some historians claim that by 1532 Cartier was a master pilot who had made trips to Brazil and Newfoundland.

The records concerning this and other matters of Cartier's life are unclear until the fall of 1533. By then, Cartier was no longer a young man. He was an experienced sea captain, respected not just among the St. Malo fishers but throughout France. He had married in 1519, but apparently little of his time was spent at home. He was almost always at sea. He was such a respected ***mariner*** that on October 31, 1533, the king of France, Francis I, gave Cartier an important mission. The captain from St. Malo was to follow up on the explorations of Cabot and the transatlantic fishing vessels. On behalf of the king, Cartier was to explore beyond Newfoundland. His goal would be to find the fabled Northwest Passage.

*King Francis I was inspired by the riches
Spaniards were bringing back from the
Caribbean and the lower Americas. He decided
France should send its own explorers across the
Atlantic on a quest for new lands.*

Gold for the King!

2

*L*ike other European monarchs of his era, France's King Francis I wanted to be the first to find the best route to the Orient, and he wanted to control this route. Jacques Cartier, the king hoped, would return with both a sampling of gold and news of a shorter route to China.

Cartier wasn't the first navigator dispatched to the New World by King Francis. In 1524 the French king had sent an Italian sailor named Giovanni da Verrazano across the Atlantic to look for the Northwest Passage. Verrazano reached what is now the eastern coast of the United States and explored more than a thousand miles of shoreline. But

Giovanni da Verrazano, sailing in the employ of the French king, explored the Atlantic coast of North America from the Carolinas past what today is New York.

he found no route to the Orient. History isn't clear, but some chroniclers believe Cartier may have even been a member of Verrazano's expedition.

Before Verrazano, other French explorers had ventured across the Atlantic: the Parmentier brothers, Thomas Aubert, and Jean Denys among them. Their attempts to break through the wild continent and establish settlements had all failed.

Cartier and his 61-man crew sailed in two small ships on April 20, 1534. Their voyage across the North Atlantic to Newfoundland, some 2,000 miles to the west, took them three weeks. The plan was to sail northward along the coast—but even as late in the year as May, the Newfoundland coastal waters proved to be filled with arctic ice. The Frenchmen had to wait impatiently in a sheltered bay for another 10 days before they could safely move northward through the melting ice.

Soon they came upon one of the natural wonders of the New World, a small island off the Newfoundland coast that the French called L'Isle des Ouaisseaulx, meaning "Isle of Birds" in English. Cartier and his men could see how the island had gotten its name. Thousands and thousands of birds of all sizes lived on the island and flew low over the surrounding waters.

"Some," Cartier recorded, "are as big as geese, and black and white, with beaks like a crow's, and they are always in the sea, without ever being able to fly, for they have small wings . . . with which they skim as quickly through the water as other birds do through the air."

These birds, which the sailors called "apponats," were unusually fat—and tasty. They provided a welcome supply of fresh meat. The birds were so thick here that hunters could gather them simply by trampling to death as many as they needed for food.

Polar bears could also be found on the frigid islands. They alarmed the observers with their size and quickness as they bounded through the surf. The French were able to kill one of the white creatures, which provided them with even more meat.

Continuing northward through a sea of awesome icebergs, they probed the bleak, rocky shoreline of what is now Labrador on the North American mainland. Then Cartier shifted his course to the southwest, entering a waterway that today is known as the Strait of Belle Isle. This strait separates the island part of Newfoundland from the Canadian mainland. It leads from the Atlantic Ocean into the broad Gulf of St. Lawrence.

After resting a few days, the expedition began skirting down the west coast of Newfoundland. It was now mid-June 1534, and Cartier was examining territory unknown to European explorers. The coast was thick with fog, and his navigational instruments were crude. But he and his men safely covered the 300 miles to the southwestern tip of Newfoundland.

Now they set out across the great gulf, heading— they hoped—toward China. They sailed past many beautiful islands; Cartier gave these islands French names. In early July, they approached a piece of land (Miscou Point) at the southern opening of a large inlet. This body of water proved to be a bay. Cartier named it Chaleur Bay. On its north side was the lower coast of a large landmass that jutted into the Gulf of St. Lawrence from the west.

The hilly land to the north, covered with green, fragrant cedar trees and other hardwoods, was found to be a *peninsula*, which later came to be called Gaspé. To the south was the fertile land of what today is New Brunswick.

At Labrador, the Frenchmen encountered a band of natives dressed in animal skins and paddling canoes made of birch tree bark. Cartier described them this way: "They knot their hair on their heads like a handful of twisted hay with a nail or some other thing passed through the middle, and woven in are the feathers of birds."

By now, the commander was beginning to understand he would find no simple route to the Orient through the islands and inlets west of Newfoundland. He still had hope, though. He saw several openings along the shoreline that he wanted to explore further, but his commission for this trip was coming to an end. He knew he soon would have to return home and report to the king.

The French had not been anchored long in Chaleur Bay when **Micmac Indians** in bark canoes approached them. The European visitors and the natives eyed each other nervously. Cartier ordered his sailors to fire cannonballs over the Indians' heads to demonstrate the power of the French ships.

A day later, the Indians offered animal furs as a sign of friendship. In return, Cartier gave them knives and other gifts. Soon, the Indians were bringing animal pelts and other items to trade for these colorful foreign curiosities.

Cartier's party did not stay long in Chaleur Bay. Weathering summer storms, they nosed northward around the peninsula, into the Gaspé Passage. Had they ventured westward, this would have led them into the mouth of the St. Lawrence River. That discovery would wait until a later voyage.

Near the northeastern point of the peninsula, they met another Indian tribe. These people spoke a different language from the other natives the Frenchmen had met earlier. Cartier later described them as scantily clothed in animal skins. They had long black ponytails stringing down from the tops of their heads, but otherwise their scalps were shaved. They ate their wild game and fish almost raw. Carti-

As Native Americans look on in the foreground, Jacques Cartier claims the Gaspé Peninsula for France in July 1534.

er added that they proved themselves to be "marvelous thieves," but he made friends with them, giving them bells and combs and other cheap items. These Indians probably were Iroquois.

At this place on July 24, the French planted a large wooden cross. On it was carved in French, "Long live the king of France!" Cartier was claiming the Gaspé Peninsula for King Francis.

When the Native Americans understood what was happening—that these intruders were trying to

In his dealings with the natives of North America, Jacques Cartier discovered a new kind of wealth to be found in the New World. It was not gold and jewels, but it was much easier to obtain: animal furs!

take possession of their land—they shouted angrily. Cartier, however, demonstrated a craftiness that would serve him well during his future exploration of the region. Rather than trying to conquer the Indians, he persuaded the chief and members of his family to come aboard his ship. There, he gave them French clothes, feasted them, and made them dizzy with wine.

Then he made a bold proposal. He asked that the chief's sons Domagaia and Taignoagny return with him to France.

Chief Donnaconna must have been startled by the invitation. After all, why would he want to watch his own children sail away with these strangers in their tall, wooden ships? They might never return.

But Cartier assured the chief he would bring the boys right back the following year. For their part, Taignoagny and Domagaia were excited and wanted to visit this place called France. Cartier lavished more gifts on the chief. The Indian leader finally agreed to let his sons go.

Why did Cartier want to take the young Indians with him? He had two reasons. First, he wanted to impress his king with these "savages." Second, he wanted the brothers to learn to speak French. Having them as interpreters, he knew, would help him in his explorations of the New World.

So the French set sail with their guests. Heading northeast, they came to what is now Anticosti Island, a large island near the entrance to the St. Lawrence Seaway. They explored halfway around the island, into the narrow *strait* that separates it from the modern-day coast of mainland Quebec. This strait is known today as the Jacques Cartier Passage.

Cartier wanted to explore further. Perhaps the water to the west of Anticosti would lead them to China. But their supplies were running low, and the end of summer was approaching. Cold weather comes early in the northland, and conditions for sea travel deteriorate. Cartier and his men did not want to be stranded on these wilderness shores until the following spring. They decided to head homeward.

Return to the New World 3

Even in warm weather, storms in the North Atlantic are frequent and often violent. In late August, Cartier's ships were caught in a tempest that rocked and drenched them for three days. The sailors feared for their lives, but the ships held up until the storm ended. The first week of September 1534, they returned safely to St. Malo.

Jacques Cartier was proving that he was different from other early explorers of North America. Many commanders of earlier expeditions had been brutal and greedy, and they had lacked navigational and naval skills. As a result, their voyages were plagued by costly errors, the needless loss of ships and supplies, ***desertion***, constant tension, and even deadly mutinies. Cartier, on the other hand, was an excellent sailor and wise leader. He let his men have a say in some of the major decisions. He was a cautious navigator.

The proof of his abilities was delivered at the end of his first expedition. Not only had both ships weathered the double Atlantic crossing; not one of his men had been lost to illness, accident, violence, or desertion.

Cartier hoped to return to the New World in the spring of 1535, if he could obtain the king's permission and support. And events turned out as he wished, partly because he made an important friend in the royal court: Admiral Philippe de Brion-Chabot. The admiral recognized the possibilities of the distant coast with its maze of coastal islands and inlets. He used his influence to help Cartier.

King Francis and his court were also impressed by the reports of Cartier's first voyage—although they were disappointed he had brought back no gold. The king called Cartier "France's pilot of the western sea." He wanted the navigator to learn more about the waters beyond Anticosti Island. Possibly, there lay the passage to China.

The king also wanted Cartier to carry out the "**Great Commission**," converting New World natives to Christianity. The French church wanted to bring the Indians into the Catholic faith.

In Europe at that time, a division was growing between the Roman Catholic Church and the **Protestants** who had broken away from Catholic practices and beliefs. Because of this, the struggle for position and power in the Americas was not just a struggle between European nations, but also between religious denominations and societies. Cartier was a steadfast Catholic—an important trait, in the eyes of King Francis. The king felt certain he could count on Cartier to help make the New World a pillar of the Catholic faith.

For all these reasons, the king approved Cartier's second voyage, which began in late May 1535. This time he had three ships and more than 100 men— including about a dozen of Cartier's relatives. The crew also included carpenters and a doctor. One of Cartier's vessels, the *L'Emerillon*, was only a small coastal **pinnace**. But the largest, *La Grande Hermine*, was an impressive 140-ton ship that had 12 cannons. In between was *La Petite Hermine*, about half the size of *La Grande Hermine*.

*This detailed French map showing Labrador, Newfound-
land, and the Gulf of St. Lawrence was made in 1699.*

As Cartier had promised, he was returning the
two Native American boys to their country. They
had learned to speak French, and they had enjoyed
their visit. The voyage back across the Atlantic, however, was anything but enjoyable. Stormy weather
damaged the ships and made the sailors miserable.
For a while, the vessels were separated, and they
needed almost two months to reach the New World.

After the French ships met in the Strait of Belle Isle, Cartier directed them through the Gulf of St. Lawrence, past Anticosti Island. After waiting out a storm in the shelter of a bay, they moved into the wide waters beyond. Cartier soon learned this was not an ocean passage, but rather the mouth of a large river. At the time, it was called the River of Hochelaga; today we know it as the St. Lawrence.

The entrance to the river was about 80 miles wide from north to south. The shoreline in these parts was awe-inspiring, with high cliffs and dense green forests. All the Frenchmen agreed: This was a land of great beauty—but also of uncertainty.

Dodging dangerous shoals, or shallows, Cartier and his party sailed up the gradually narrowing river for about 500 miles. They saw whales, seals, and walruses in the water, many kinds of birds, and both large and small furry game in the woods.

In time, they came to an island covered by wild grapevines. More than 20 miles long and about 7 miles wide, it was separated

Up the St. Lawrence River, the Indian guides told Cartier, was a sprawling land they knew as *Canada*. This was the Native American word for "village."

An encounter between Native Americans and a group of Frenchmen in small boats is depicted in this painting entitled "Cartier Discovers the St. Lawrence."

from the northern shore by a narrow channel. The Indian guides told Cartier the land across from the island was called *Kebec*, meaning "narrow." Today, the city of Quebec is situated there. Cartier named the small body of land the Isle of Orlean, after one of King Francis's sons.

Nearby was the Iroquois village of Stadacona. The Native Americans living there wore feathers in their long, black hair and painted their bodies with colored clay. Their appearance made the visitors nervous, but the Indians turned out to be friendly. Cartier and his men served Chief Donnaconna a fabulous meal aboard the flagship, and the Indians treated the Frenchmen to a feast of their own.

The French enjoyed the event. They ate the meat of bear and beaver that the Indians supplied, and they were amused when Donnaconna told of monsters and ghosts that dwelled further upriver. Apparently, the chief was trying to discourage them from continuing.

Cartier was not frightened by the stories. He set some of his men to work building a fort on the river-bank, where they would spend the coming winter. Then he and the others headed upstream in the smallest ship and some of their longboats. This river would obviously not provide a short route to the Orient. Nevertheless, Cartier wanted to explore it as far as he could.

He was impressed by the river's green shores. The woods teemed with wildlife: moose, elk, bear, beaver, deer, and many varieties of birds. Wild grapes were plentiful, and the trees were tall and straight—useful for shipbuilding. Cartier called them "the finest trees in the world."

They made friends with the Indians they met, trading them trinkets and knives for fish. The "savages" or "wild men," as the French called them, were strong and fearless. At one point, a single native reportedly picked up the French commander and "carried him on shore as easily as if he had been a six-year-old child."

After about a month, they came to a large Indian village called Hochelaga built on an island in the river at the foot of a mountain. Cartier named the mountain *Mont Réal*, or "Royal Mountain." Today, it is the site of the city of Montreal. In Cartier's day, however, a circular wooden fence protected the settlement. The houses inside were about 100 feet long and were sectioned into large rooms. Several families lived in each house. Fires for cooking and warmth burned in the center of each dwelling.

The Indians of this settlement were also friendly. For five days they feasted Cartier and his men. They treated the French leader as if he were a god, but Cartier did not encourage this. Instead, he told them about Christianity, and he read to them from the Gospel of John in the New Testament.

Meanwhile, the Indians introduced tobacco to the French. The tobacco leaves were smoked in long pipes. "They say it keeps them warm and in good health," Cartier recorded. He wanted to learn for himself what it was like to smoke. But when he inhaled, the tobacco burned his mouth like pepper. Cartier and his men also tried Indian bread, called *carracony*, which the natives made from corn.

The Indians told Cartier and his men that nearby rivers led to a "freshwater sea." Thus, Cartier and his men learned for the first time of the enormous bodies of water we call the *Great Lakes*.

Upstream from Mont Réal, the Frenchmen discovered several miles of dangerous rapids, where rocks churned the river into whitewater. The rapids made boat travel impossible; canoes and other lightweight watercraft had to be *portaged*—carried on land to smooth water. Today this area is known as the Lachine Rapids.

Autumn had come by now, and already the air was cold. Cartier and his men said good-bye to their Native American friends at Hochelaga and began the journey back downstream to Kebec. On their way they stocked a supply of wild game to take to the fort. There they would wait out their first winter in the New World.

Winter
in the
Wilderness

Cartier offers a crucifix to Chief Donnaconna; a French fort is in the background. To survive the winter at Kebec, the French needed the friendship of the Iroquois.

4

Cartier's men back at Kebec had built a fine fortress by the time the river party returned. Cold autumn winds were beginning to blow down from the Arctic, but the settlers were ready for winter. They had erected huts within the fort's spiked walls, set up stoves brought ashore from the ships, and gathered supplies.

By December, blizzards piled snow high against the fortress walls, and the river froze around the anchored ships. Even if the French had wanted to return to France, now they could not leave. They were resolved to discover for themselves what winter was like in this new land. Already, they could tell it would be much harsher than in northern France.

During the winter, Cartier and Chief Donnaconna often visited each other. As a gesture of goodwill, Donnaconna allowed three Iroquois children to stay with the Europeans, hoping to persuade Cartier not to establish contacts with the Iroquois's enemies. In return for the children, Cartier offered two swords and two brass chamberpots to Chief Donnaconna. Although the Frenchmen and the Indians treated each other with respect, they were watchful and always suspicious.

Relations between the French and the Indians deteriorated during the winter months. Taignoagny and Domagaia, the two brothers Cartier had taken with him to France, informed the Indian community that the French had taken advantage of them by trading worthless trinkets for valuable supplies. The Indians were further angered by Cartier's refusal to return the three children Donnaconna had sent him.

The settlement had other troubles as well. When they ran out of fresh meat, the French were forced to live on hard corn and salted meat. They had no green vegetables or fruit. As a result, a disease called *scurvy* began to spread through the huts. Scurvy is caused by a shortage of vitamins. Because of the lack of fresh fruits and vegetables, the men developed sores all over their bodies. Their limbs became swollen and discolored, and they began to lose their teeth.

The harshness of the winter came as a surprise to the French. They knew that Kebec was situated slightly farther south than St. Malo, their home port. They had assumed that Kebec therefore would enjoy a climate no more severe than that of France.

Scurvy can be cured—and it can be prevented with wise nutrition. But with no way to correct the situation, some of the men became dangerously sick. They also developed other diseases . . . and some began to die. By late winter, two dozen people had died, and all but 10, including Cartier, were too sick to get out of bed.

From the natives, however, the settlers learned that scurvy could be treated with a kind of tea made by boiling the bark and needles of a certain tree the Indians called *annedda* (probably a variety of spruce

This detail from the Portulan Map of the New World, drawn sometime between 1536 and 1542, shows Cartier and his followers in Canada.

or cedar). Two native women chopped the branches from a nearby tree and brought it to the fort, and the handful of healthy men in Cartier's company brewed up a pot of the medicine. Astonishingly, Cartier reported, his sick men recovered in a week.

Gradually, spring arrived, and the ice and snow slowly thawed. Now Cartier's expedition could return to France. But because he had fewer men after the winter's deaths, he decided to break up *La*

Petite Hermine rather than try to sail home short-handed. He planned what he would report to the king about their discoveries.

Chief Donnaconna had told Cartier that gold and other colorful minerals were to be found in certain parts of the wilderness. Particularly intriguing was a woodland kingdom the Indians called Saguenay. The stories said it was a land rich not just in gold and jewels but also in copper and other important minerals. Cartier knew this was the kind of news King Francis liked to hear. He also knew the stories would be more believable if the king heard them directly from Chief Donnaconna rather than from Cartier or from a young Indian captive.

So in May 1536 Cartier made a grave decision—one that was to hurt French and Indian relations for many years to come. He had his men take the chief, his two sons, and a few other Indians captive. Then they quickly boarded their ships and set off downstream. Cartier promised the tribe he would bring their chief safely home to them the next year. But the Indians were furious. And as time would prove, Cartier's next voyage would be delayed . . . until it was too late for Chief Donnaconna.

The Long
Delay

The harbor at St. Malo, home of Jacques Cartier. After Cartier returned to France to report his discoveries to the king, he was unable to return to Canada for six years.

5

ailing homeward across the ocean, Cartier thought of his next voyage to the New World. He knew the leaders of France and other European countries hoped to find wealth there. Cartier, however, realized this wild and beautiful land was far more valuable than any gold it might contain. Its green hills supported the Native Americans well; these fertile lands could also support French colonists. Poor, landless French farmers at home might find a new and far better life across the sea. Here also was excellent fishing, plentiful wild game, excellent soil for planting, grassland for cattle, and thick forests with every kind of wood needed to build homes, boats, and tools.

The voyage home was a pleasant one. In mid-July, Cartier's ships, carrying the surviving French sailors and their native captives, anchored in St. Malo's harbor.

The situation in France was not so pleasant. War loomed between France and neighboring Spain. The two countries would soon be fighting each other. Because of this, King Francis would have no money, men, or ships to to spare for a third voyage— at any rate, not for a long while. In fact, many months passed before the king even found time to see Cartier and listen to the reports he and Chief Donnaconna brought from the New World.

Cartier's old friend, Admiral Brion-Chabot, had lost favor in the king's court. And soon, a Spanish army invaded across the southern French border. Events seemed to conspire to prevent Cartier from returning to explore the St. Lawrence River.

Realizing he would be making no third trip to the New World for a long time, Cartier took *La*

An illustration of Cartier's ship, La Grande Hermine. *With France involved in a war with Spain, Cartier had to postpone his return to the New World. Instead, he sailed out into the Atlantic Ocean to fish and attack Spanish ships.*

Grande Hermine into the Atlantic and became a **privateer** for France, raiding Spanish and Portuguese vessels. Privateers operated in the service of their countries, but otherwise, they were little more respectable than pirates.

During the next four years, while Cartier captured enemy ships and resumed his fishing career on the blue ocean, Donnaconna and the other Native Americans languished and died in France.

The Treaty of Nice in 1538 brought the war between France and Spain to a close. In October 1540, Cartier at last received the king's commission to return to the New World for the third time. But there was a complication. King Francis chose a French nobleman named Jean-François de La Rocque, Sieur de Roberval, to be the leader of this expedition. Roberval was to be the governor of French lands in the New World. Cartier was named captain-general under him. Roberval had experience as an army commander, but he had never sailed on the deep sea. Now he was given authority over the lifelong mariner and proven explorer Cartier.

> Roberval's plan was to colonize the territories of Newfoundland and St. Lawrence. He would divide and sell the land to French farmers, and reap the lion's share of whatever wealth these settlers would obtain.

Why? Because of Roberval's social standing. Noblemen were all-powerful, even though they often knew less than "common" folk like Cartier.

Cartier was given five ships (Roberval would have additional vessels) and enough supplies to last two years, including cattle, hogs, and other livestock. Priests accompanied the expedition, prepared to convert the Native Americans to Christianity. The king enticed French adventurers to join the group by promising them land in the New World.

News of the cold, sickness, and uncertainty of life abroad, however, made recruiting sailors difficult. So the French leaders looked to prisoners as able-bodied seamen. This expedition would include some of the most notorious criminals in France.

Cartier sailed on May 23, 1541. Roberval's own men, including the expedition's soldiers, were not yet ready to leave. In fact, Roberval did not cross the Atlantic with his four ships until a year later.

Later that summer, Cartier reunited with the Indians at Stadacona. The French leader admitted to them that Chief Donnaconna was dead—but he told them falsely that their other tribesmen had chosen to remain in France, marry, and become French noblemen. Cartier was afraid that if he broke the news that all the Indians had died in France, he would have a terrible fight on his hands.

The Iroquois made no trouble, but Cartier doubted they believed his lie. Apparently, they spread word along the river that the French could not be trusted. Problems with the Indians intensified during the rest of Cartier's stay in the New World.

Cartier proceeded up the St. Lawrence. At a place called Cap Rouge, he anchored his ships. Around them was a bountiful forest, and they found deposits of gold-colored ore, iron, and "stones like diamonds." They built two forts, one at the base of a high cliff and the other at the top. Cartier called this settlement Charlesbourg Royal.

The Frenchmen started to clear fields and plant crops. They shipped back to France a supply of the minerals they discovered. Cartier himself then went to look for the fabled kingdom of Saguenay.

While searching for the legendary land of riches, Cartier also hoped to improve relations between the French and Native Americans. To make up for taking Iroquois to France—sometimes against their will—he now placed two French boys in the care of a trusted chief at a place called Achelacy. The boys' job was to learn the Iroquois language thoroughly. This would help the French learn more about the New World through the eyes of the Indians.

Stopped again by the Lachine Rapids and other river obstacles above Mont Réal, Cartier visited briefly with friendly Indians. Then he began to return downriver. At Achelacy, however, he saw that trouble was brewing. Most of the Indians had deserted the village. Cartier learned that some of the tribes were conspiring to attack the French.

As he continued back to Charlesbourg Royal,

the dangerous state of affairs became more obvious. Indians always had been welcomed at the French settlements, and they came and went freely among the Europeans. But now they were avoiding the Charlesbourg Royal colony. Worse, Cartier received word that a large group of natives had gathered at Stadacona. Fearing a ferocious Indian attack, Cartier ordered the fort at Charlesbourg Royal to be made stronger and careful watch to be kept at all times.

In the end, the Indians did not unleash a full-scale assault against the French. But they carried out small raids almost every day. More than 30 of Cartier's men were killed.

The Iroquois threat kept the colonists confined to the fort at Charlesbourg Royal throughout the winter of

What caused the sudden hostility between the Indians and French? Historians aren't sure, but some of the Frenchmen may have been treating the natives badly. After all, many of the colonists were lifelong criminals. When Cartier and his officers were not around to keep them in line, they took what they wanted and did as they pleased. They felt no need to behave themselves as honorable guests in the territory of the "savages."

The fighting between the French settlers at Charlesbourg Royal and the local natives was fierce. This drawing from a 16th-century French book about the settlement in Canada shows an Iroquois scalping a white man.

1541–42. Meanwhile, the dreaded scurvy ravaged the forts. This time, the French knew how to cure the disease with the cedar mixture, but the winter was still a horrible season for the explorers. The temperatures were so cold that inside the barracks water froze in buckets only a few feet away from the stoves, which were kept blazing at all times. Snow and frigid wind whooshed loudly around the walls day and night.

By spring, Cartier had had enough. In June 1542, he and his men left the fort at Charlesbourg Royal.

They sailed back down the St. Lawrence River, into the Gulf of St. Lawrence. Off Newfoundland, in what is now the harbor at St. John's, they met the ships of the commander Roberval.

Roberval could not understand why Cartier had abandoned Charlesbourg Royal. He ordered the captain to return upriver, despite Cartier's protests that the Iroquois were on a deadly warpath. Cartier knew better than to return, though. He knew his men would resist, and he himself was weary of the cold wilderness. He disobeyed Roberval's order.

Cartier's ships slipped away by night and made for the open Atlantic.

Return to France

After leaving Canada in 1542, Jacques Cartier, pictured standing on the deck of his ship, never returned to the St. Lawrence River.

6

*A*board his vessels, Cartier was transporting to the king many barrels of minerals—gold and jewels he thought would please the court. But when he arrived home in October 1542, the king's officials examined the "treasure" and announced that Cartier had been deceived. (Or perhaps he was the deceiver.) What Cartier said was gold actually was **iron pyrite**—"fool's gold." What he thought were diamonds were only pieces of quartz.

Despite his embarrassment, Cartier's friends and family at St. Malo treated him with great respect. They were proud of his skills as a navigator and his accomplishments as an explorer of the incredible New World.

As a reward for his efforts, King Francis gave Cartier two of the ships he had used on his voyage. Cartier was able to live out the rest of his life in comfort and happiness—quite unlike most New World explorers of his day, many of whom died violently, penniless, or imprisoned. He was the guest of honor at weddings and other social events in St. Malo. Veteran sailors often gathered at his country estate on the coast of Brittany at Limoilou, or his home in St. Malo. There they reminisced about their adventures on the high seas. Cartier's friend Sebastian Cabot, the son of John Cabot and also an explorer of the New World, is said to have been present at some of these storytelling sessions.

Back along the St. Lawrence River, after Cartier deserted him, Roberval decided to try his own hand at building a colony. He had his men construct an impressive new fort at Charlesbourg Royal—which Roberval now called France-Roy. There, they spent the following winter.

Roberval's party included some of the first French women to arrive in America. The expedition also included well-to-do Frenchmen who had come along in hopes of finding wealth in the New World; these men were unprepared for a life of hardship in the wilderness. To make matters worse, Roberval was a cruel leader, severely punishing anyone who complained.

Not surprisingly, the winter of 1542–43 was a nightmare for Roberval's settlement. Those who survived the disease that swept through the fort nearly starved to death. To help conserve food supplies, Roberval declared that three days a week were "fast days"–meaning people were not allowed to eat. Many of the poor citizens of France-Roy were dead by springtime. Conditions were so bad that the Indians, forgetting their resentment, felt sorry for the Europeans.

After the spring thaw, Roberval and some of his men explored a short way up the St. Lawrence and the other rivers that emptied into it. Soon, however, they gave up and returned to France. The Native Americans, once friendly, had been soured by the Frenchmen's mistreatment and were pleased to see them sail away.

A rescue ship, meanwhile, had been sent from France to relieve Roberval's expedition. Some historians believe that Cartier himself commanded the ship. If true, Cartier never wrote about the voyage or recorded whether he actually met the homecoming colonists. We do know that one way or another Roberval reached home safely. He died in France in 1561, a victim of the civil and religious strife that dominated the country at that time.

Jacques Cartier died near St. Malo on September 1, 1557. Today, no one is certain exactly what this great explorer looked like. Although there are many portraits of him, all are based on second-hand descriptions and speculation. However, Cartier is celebrated as a brave explorer and sailor who opened a large area of North America to eventual European settlement.

* * * *

European rulers still hoped that the coveted Northwest Passage existed. However, none of the French or English explorers so far had found it. Nor had they found any river or strait that promised to lead to a western ocean. A later generation would have to prove—or disprove—the theory of the "short route to the Orient."

Native Americans bring furs to trade with the French.
Although Cartier and other French explorers did not find
gold in North America, the land's natural resources were
a valuable discovery.

After King Francis I, French leaders for many years did not want to send costly expeditions to the New World. The Spanish were bringing home entire convoys of treasures stolen from native kingdoms in the lower Americas, but Cartier and others who explored the cold northern regions had found almost nothing of value to the French court. The only French transatlantic mariners were the fishermen who continued to reap a good living from the

The great French explorer Samuel de Champlain followed up on Cartier's discoveries. In the early 17th century he traveled up the St. Lawrence, founding the French settlement of Quebec in 1608.

dense schools of cod swimming in the Grand Banks. These sailors developed one of the real sources of wealth in the New World. Cartier had seen this, but he had not taken time to study its potential. He was too busy searching for the Northwest Passage.

In trading with the natives of Newfoundland and the lower coasts, the French fishermen began bringing home more and more animal skins. Thick fur hides were very valuable to Europeans, who used them to make luxurious coats and hats. In the great wilderness across the sea, furry animals were everywhere to be found: bear, fox, deer and elk, otter, and especially beaver. This new form of wealth was a type of trade that seems cruel and bloody today— and in fact is banned in many countries.

By the end of the 1500s, the French government had decided to support expeditions to colonize what is today eastern Canada. But early attempts at permanent settlement continued to be fatal disasters, for the New World was indeed a savage land, and northern winters were terribly cold. When settlements finally did begin to take firm footholds, their inhabitants had to endure many hardships with few pleasures.

One of the greatest French explorers of Canada would cross the ocean about half a century after Cartier's death. He was Samuel de Champlain. Backed by King Henry IV and later by King Louis XIII, he explored the St. Lawrence region in the early 1600s. Champlain founded the city of Quebec in 1608. It was the first European settlement in Canada to withstand the tribulations of the frontier.

Champlain and his men later pushed further westward into the vast country, reaching the Great Lakes. He spent his life planning the colonization of New France, as Canada was called. Champlain, not Cartier, is the man whom historians remember as "the Father of New France."

Nevertheless, Cartier earned an important place in the history of New World discovery. He had probed the Gaspé coast and the St. Lawrence River, established ties with many of the Indians and learned to communicate with them, and brought back to France detailed descriptions of this promising land across the ocean. In the port of St. Malo— known throughout Europe as the home of daring, savvy seafarers—Jacques Cartier would be forever the master mariner.

1491 Jacques Cartier is born in the port of St. Malo, France.

1492 Columbus, searching for a westward route to the East Indies, discovers the Americas.

1497 English sea captain John Cabot sails to Newfoundland. Cabot disappears while attempting to return to Newfoundland the next year.

1534 Cartier's first expedition arrives at Newfoundland in May. He meets the Micmac Indians, claims the Gaspé Peninsula for France, and returns to St. Malo in September.

1535 Cartier's second expedition begins in May. He earns his place in history as the first European to explore what is today the great St. Lawrence River.

1536 After spending a miserable winter in Canada, Cartier returns to find France on the brink of war with Spain.

1541 In May Cartier sails from St. Malo on his third New World expedition. His commander, Roberval, will follow a year later.

1542 Cartier arrives home from his last expedition in October. He has failed once again to discover riches or a short route to the Orient.

1557 Cartier dies near St. Malo on September 1.

1608 Samuel de Champlain establishes the city of Quebec in New France.

Glossary

carracony–Indian cornbread.

corsairs–French pirates or privateers.

desertion–the loss of soldiers or expedition members who quit or leave without permission.

galleons–heavy, square-rigged sailing ships of the 15th to early 18th centuries, used for war or commerce, especially by the Spanish.

Grand Banks–waters rich with codfish located off the coast of Newfoundland.

Great Commission–Christ's direction to his followers to spread the Gospel throughout the world. Nations have often used the Great Commission to serve their own ends.

Great Lakes–five connected freshwater lakes bordering the United States and Canada, including Lakes Superior, Huron, Michigan, Erie, and Ontario.

iron pyrite–a worthless yellow mineral formed from sulphur and iron, sometimes called "fool's gold."

Iroquois confederacy–an alliance of Native American tribes in New York and lower Canada that consisted of the Cayuga, Mohawk, Oneida, Onondaga, and Seneca peoples.

mariner–one who navigates or assists in the navigation of a ship; in other words, a seaman or sailor.

Micmac Indians–welcoming and friendly tribe who were the first Indians encountered by the French in Chaleur Bay.

Mont Réal–Originally an Indian village called Hochelaga, or present-day Montreal.

Northwest Passage–the sought-after shortcut through the New
World to China and the Orient, to facilitate trade in
valuable spices and silk.

peninsula–a land area surrounded on three sides by water.

pinnace–a small ship, usually used to sail in coastal waters, that
can be taken apart easily and stored in the hold of a
larger vessel.

portage–Indian term referring to the act of carrying canoes and
small boats over land, to avoid rapids and falls in order
to reach smooth waters.

privateer–a ship owner who is authorized by the government of
his country to attack enemy vessels.

Protestants–members of a religious movement in Europe that
broke away from the Roman Catholic Church.

province–a region of a country, usually separated from other
provinces for geographical or political reasons.

scurvy–disease caused by vitamin C deficiency. Symptoms
include bleeding gums, loose teeth, aching joints, and
internal bleeding. If untreated, it can lead to death.

spices–any of various aromatic vegetable products, such as pepper or nutmeg, used to season or flavor foods. Spices
were rare and highly valued in 16th-century Europe.

strait–a relatively narrow passageway that connects two large
bodies of water.

Further Reading

Averill, Esther. *Cartier Sails the St. Lawrence.* New York: Harper & Brothers, 1956.

Brenner, Barbara. *If You Were There in 1492.* New York: Aladdin Paperbacks, 1998.

Coulter, Tony. *Jacques Cartier, Samuel de Champlain, and the French Explorers of Canada.* New York and Philadelphia: Chelsea House Publishers, 1993.

Dor-Ner, Zvi. *Columbus and the Age of Discovery.* New York: William Morrow, 1992.

Edmonds, Walter D. *The Musket and the Cross.* Boston: Little, Brown and Company, 1968.

Harmon, Daniel E. *La Salle and the Exploration of the Mississippi.* Philadelphia: Chelsea House Publishers, 2001.

Hynson, Colin. *Columbus and the Renaissance Explorers.* Hauppauge, NY: Barron's Educational Series, Inc., 1998.

Konstam, August. *Historical Atlas of Exploration, 1492-1600.* New York: Checkmark Books, 2000.

Mason, Antony, and Keith Lye. *The Children's Atlas of Exploration: Follow in the Footsteps of the Great Explorers.* Brookfield, CT: Millbrook Press, 1993.

Syme, Ronald. *Cartier: Finder of the St. Lawrence.* New York: William Morrow and Company, 1958.

Picture Credits

DANIEL E. HARMON is an editor and writer living in Spartanburg, South Carolina. He has written several books on humor and history, and has contributed historical and cultural articles to the *New York Times, Music Journal, Nautilus,* and many other periodicals. He is the managing editor of *Sandlapper: The Magazine of South Carolina* and is editor of *The Lawyer's PC* newsletter. His books include *Civil War Leaders* and *Fighting Units of the American War of Independence.*